Trea

ROSH

HASHANAH

25 STORIES THAT IGNITE FAITH IN THE JEWISH NEW YEAR!

CONTACT:
Judah Joy Press
1234 Elmwood Avenue, Suite 567
Los Angeles, CA 90028
United States
Contact Email:
info@judahjoypress.com

- Table of Content -

CHAPTER ONE

Ari and the Golden Apple

Ari, a curious little boy who adored exploring the world around him, resided in a small village encircled by a lush forest brimming with secrets and adventures waiting to be uncovered. Many afternoons were spent by Ari wandering through the tall trees, listening to the birds sing, and envisioning all sorts of magical creatures concealed in the shadows.

One sunny day, shortly before Rosh Hashanah, Ari embarked on one of his typical adventures. Venturing deeper into the forest, he observed something out of the ordinary. Amid the fallen leaves and beneath a bush, something shiny captured his attention. It was a golden apple, gleaming brightly in the sunlight, as though it was beckoning to him.

Ari's heart raced with excitement at the sight before him, unlike anything he had ever seen. Gently, he reached down, picked up the apple, and felt its warmth in his hands, almost as if it pulsed with life. Turning it over, he admired its smooth, golden exterior. Suddenly, to Ari's amazement, the apple spoke!

Ari and the Golden Apple

"Hello, Ari," it uttered in a soft, melodious voice. "I am a special apple, here to impart upon you the significance of new beginnings."

Astonishment filled Ari. "How can an apple possibly teach me something?" he inquired, his eyes wide with wonder and curiosity.

The apple elucidated, "Every year, during Rosh Hashanah, we commemorate the commencement of a new year. It is a time for introspection, seeking forgiveness, and planning for a better future. By partaking of me, you will be reminded that regardless of the past, you can always start anew."

Reflecting on moments of impatience with his younger sister, times of neglecting his parents, and the minor errors made throughout the year, Ari acknowledged his capacity for improvement. With a deep breath, Ari took a small, hesitant bite of the golden apple.

Instantly, a warm, comforting sensation coursed through his body. It was as though the apple's enchantment infused him with fresh hope and insight. Ari realized that each day presented a new opportunity to show kindness, patience, and thoughtfulness. A sense of weightlessness overcame him as if a burden had been lifted from his heart.

Ari and the Golden Apple

As Ari absorbed the apple's message, its glow gradually dimmed. "Thank you," Ari murmured, placing the apple gently on the ground. With one final shimmer, the apple vanished into the earth, leaving behind a profound peace and a revitalized resolve in Ari's heart.

Hurrying home, Ari was eager to impart his newfound wisdom to his family. That evening, while dipping apples in honey, Ari shared the tale of the golden apple and its profound lesson. His family listened attentively, proud of the enlightenment Ari had gained.

Since that day, Ari commemorated the golden apple every Rosh Hashanah. He understood that each new year presented a precious opportunity for growth, forgiveness, and personal betterment. Thus, with every Rosh Hashanah that arrived, Ari approached the new year with optimism, knowing that regardless of the past, he could always embark on a fresh start and make the upcoming year the greatest one yet.

Moral: Regardless of past events, each new beginning offers a chance for improvement and better decision-making.

CHAPTER TWO

Sara and the Sweet Honey

Sara was eagerly looking forward to Rosh Hashanah, her favorite time of the year. She adored everything about the holiday—the family gatherings, the special prayers, and most of all, the delicious tradition of dipping apples in honey. The sweetness of the honey always brought a smile to her face, and she couldn't wait to once again share the joy with her family.

One afternoon, a few days before Rosh Hashanah, Sara decided to visit her grandmother, who lived in a cozy cottage at the edge of the village. Her grandmother's garden was full of blooming flowers and buzzing bees, and Sara loved spending time there, helping with the plants and listening to her grandmother's stories.

As they sat together in the garden, enjoying the warm afternoon sun, Sara's grandmother handed her a small jar of honey. It was golden and thick, freshly harvested from the beehives in the garden. "Do you know why we eat honey on Rosh Hashanah?" her grandmother asked, her eyes twinkling with warmth.

Sara thought for a moment. "Because it's sweet?" she guessed, remembering the taste that she loved so much.

Sara and the Sweet Honey

Her grandmother smiled and nodded. "Yes, it's sweet, but there's more to it than just the taste. Honey symbolizes the hope for a sweet and joyful year ahead. It reminds us to look for sweetness in every moment, no matter how small, and to share that sweetness with others."

Sara listened carefully, trying to understand the deeper meaning behind the tradition. She had always enjoyed the honey because it tasted good, but now she realized it was also a reminder of something more important—finding and spreading joy and kindness throughout the year.

Her grandmother continued, "When we dip the apple in honey, we're not just enjoying a treat. We're making a wish for the year to come, hoping that it will be filled with as much sweetness as the honey. And just like the bees work hard to create the honey, we too must work to bring sweetness into our lives and the lives of others."

Sara thought about her grandmother's words as she dipped an apple slice into the honey. The taste was even more delicious now that she understood its significance. She felt a warm, happy feeling in her heart, knowing that by spreading sweetness and kindness, she could make the world a better place.

Sara and the Sweet Honey

That evening, as her family gathered to celebrate Rosh Hashanah, Sara decided to do something special. She spent the afternoon baking honey cakes with her grandmother, carefully mixing the ingredients and shaping the dough. When the cakes were ready, she wrapped them up and delivered them to her neighbors, sharing the sweetness of Rosh Hashanah with everyone around her.

As she watched the smiles light up their faces, Sara realized that her grandmother was right. The true sweetness of the holiday wasn't just in the honey; it was in the joy and love she could share with others. From that day on, Sara made it her mission to spread kindness and sweetness wherever she went, not just during Rosh Hashanah, but all year long.

Moral: True sweetness comes from sharing joy and kindness with others, making the world a better place.

CHAPTER THREE

David and the Shofar

David had always been fascinated by the shofar, the ram's horn that was blown during Rosh Hashanah to mark the beginning of the new year. The powerful sound of the shofar resonated deep within him, and every year, he eagerly waited for the moment when it would be blown in the synagogue. This year, David had decided he wanted to learn how to blow the shofar himself so that he could participate in the tradition and help awaken the hearts and souls of his community.

David's grandfather, who had been blowing the shofar for many years, agreed to teach him. Every day after school, David would go to his grandfather's house to practice. His grandfather was patient and encouraging, explaining that blowing the shofar wasn't just about making a sound—it was about using the sound to inspire and uplift the spirit.

David listened carefully and tried his best, but no matter how hard he blew into the shofar, all he could produce was a weak, sputtering noise. Day after day, David practiced, but the results were always the same. He began to feel frustrated and discouraged, on the verge of giving up.

David and the Shofar

One afternoon, as David sat on the porch with the shofar in his lap, his grandfather came and sat beside him. "Don't give up, David," his grandfather said gently. "The shofar isn't just about making noise. It's about waking up our hearts and souls to the new year. Sometimes, it takes time to learn how to do something important. The sound will come when you're ready."

David nodded, trying to hold back his tears. He didn't want to disappoint his grandfather, so he decided to keep practicing. Each day, he returned to the porch and tried again, blowing into the shofar with all his might. And slowly, little by little, the sound began to change. It grew stronger, clearer, and more confident.

Finally, on the day before Rosh Hashanah, David blew into the shofar, and a clear, strong sound filled the air. It was a beautiful, resonant tone that echoed through the village. David's heart swelled with pride and joy as he realized that his persistence had paid off.

On Rosh Hashanah, David stood beside his grandfather in the synagogue, holding the shofar in his hands. When the time came, David took a deep breath and blew the shofar, filling the room with its powerful sound. As the notes rang out, he saw the people around him close their eyes in reflection, their hearts touched by the call to start the new year with renewed spirit and determination.

David and the Shofar

David smiled, knowing that he had truly awakened their hearts for the new year. He had learned that with patience, perseverance, and a little bit of faith, anything was possible.

Moral: Patience and perseverance lead to success, especially in matters of the heart and spirit.

CHAPTER FOUR

Miriam and Friends in the Orchard

Miriam resided in a quaint village surrounded by vast fields and orchards, where the air was perpetually filled with the sweet scent of ripening fruit. With Rosh Hashanah drawing near, the orchard near Miriam's abode brimmed with juicy, red apples—perfect for picking and sharing with family and friends.

One crisp, sunny afternoon, Miriam and her companions resolved to venture to the orchard to collect apples for the holiday. Their excitement was palpable, fueled by their love for apples and the knowledge that these apples would be dipped in honey during the Rosh Hashanah meal—a tradition symbolizing the wish for a sweet and prosperous new year.

Upon entering the orchard, the group of children found themselves in awe of the sight that greeted them. The trees were laden with fruit, their branches bowing under the weight of the apples. The children promptly set to work, scaling the trees, stretching for the highest branches, and meticulously choosing the ripest, juiciest apples they could lay their hands on. Laughter and chatter reverberated through the air as they collaborated, relishing each other's company and the splendor of the day.

Miriam and Friends in the Orchard

Amidst the picking, Miriam recalled her mother's teachings about Rosh Hashanah. "It's a time to contemplate the past year and ponder how we can improve in the year ahead," her mother had imparted. "It's also a time to be compassionate and magnanimous, sharing our blessings with others."

Inspired by her mother's wisdom, Miriam rallied her friends and proposed her idea. "Why don't we take some of these apples and distribute them to the villagers who may not have any?" she suggested. "It would be a lovely way to spread the joy of Rosh Hashanah."

Her friends readily agreed. Divvying up the apples they had gathered into small baskets, they adorned each one with leaves and flowers from the orchard. Together, they traversed the village, presenting the baskets to their neighbors. The children knocked on doors, offering the apples with broad smiles and heartfelt wishes for a sweet new year.

The villagers were elated by the children's benevolence. Some welcomed them in for a snack, while others expressed their gratitude with embraces and well-wishes. On their way back to the orchard, Miriam and her friends basked in a profound sense of joy and satisfaction. Not only had they harvested apples for their own families, but they had also disseminated the essence of Rosh Hashanah throughout their community.

Miriam and Friends in the Orchard

Upon returning home that evening, Miriam recounted the day's escapade to her parents. Her mother beamed and embraced her tenderly. "I'm immensely proud of you, Miriam," she remarked. "You have grasped the true essence of Rosh Hashanah—unity, generosity, and the endeavor to enhance the world."

Gathered around the table that night, dipping their apples in honey and rejoicing in the new year, Miriam realized that this Rosh Hashanah would be etched in her memory forever. The sweetness of the apples transcended their flavor to encapsulate the joy they had bestowed upon others.

Moral: Collaboration and altruism not only bring happiness but also fortify communal bonds, fostering a better world.

CHAPTER FIVE

Jacob and the Tashlich River

Jacob was a thoughtful boy who often worried about the mistakes he made. As Rosh Hashanah approached, he felt a bit uneasy. Over the past year, there had been moments when he had spoken harshly to his friends, ignored his chores, or forgotten to help his younger sister when she needed him. The thought of these mistakes weighed heavily on his mind, and he wasn't sure how to make things right.

One evening, Jacob's father noticed that his son seemed troubled. "Is something bothering you, Jacob?" he asked gently.

Jacob hesitated, then nodded. "I've made some mistakes this year, and I don't know how to fix them," he admitted.

His father smiled kindly. "Rosh Hashanah is the perfect time to let go of those mistakes and start fresh," he said. "There's a special tradition called Tashlich that helps us do just that. Why don't we go to the river tomorrow and perform Tashlich together?"

Jacob and the Tashlich River

Jacob agreed, curious about what Tashlich involved. The next afternoon, Jacob and his father walked to the nearby river, carrying a small bag of breadcrumbs. As they reached the water's edge, Jacob's father explained the ceremony.

"These breadcrumbs represent the mistakes we've made over the past year," his father said, holding out the bag. "When we cast them into the river, we're letting go of those mistakes and making a promise to do better in the year ahead."

Jacob took the bag and stood by the water, reflecting on the moments he wished he could undo. He thought about the times he had been unkind, the times he hadn't been patient, and the times he had ignored the needs of others. One by one, he took the breadcrumbs and gently tossed them into the river. As the breadcrumbs floated away, carried by the current, Jacob felt as if a weight was being lifted from his heart.

When they had finished, Jacob and his father sat by the river for a while, watching the water flow. The quietness of the moment gave Jacob time to think about the new year that was just beginning. He realized that, like the breadcrumbs disappearing into the river, his mistakes were now behind him. He could start fresh, with a clear mind and a heart full of hope.

Jacob and the Tashlich River

As they walked home, Jacob felt a sense of peace and renewal. He knew that while he couldn't change the past, he could make better choices in the future. He promised himself that he would be more mindful of his actions, kinder to his friends and family, and more helpful to those around him.

That evening, as Jacob's family gathered for the Rosh Hashanah meal, he felt lighter and happier. He understood that Rosh Hashanah wasn't just about celebrating; it was about reflecting, letting go, and looking forward to the possibilities of the new year. And with that realization, Jacob felt ready to embrace the new year with open arms.

Moral: It's important to let go of mistakes, reflect on them, and focus on improving ourselves for the future.

CHAPTER SIX

Leah and the New Clothes

Leah was thrilled as she tried on her new dress for Rosh Hashanah. It was a beautiful shade of blue, with delicate embroidery around the collar and sleeves. Leah twirled in front of the mirror, admiring how the dress swirled around her. She couldn't wait to show it off to her friends and family during the holiday celebrations.

Her mother watched with a smile as Leah beamed with happiness. "You look wonderful, Leah," she said. "But remember, Rosh Hashanah isn't just about looking good on the outside. It's also a time to think about how we can start fresh on the inside."

Leah paused and turned to her mother. "What do you mean, start fresh on the inside?" she asked.

Her mother sat down beside her and explained, "Rosh Hashanah is the beginning of the Jewish New Year. It's a time when we think about the past year—our actions, our words, and our thoughts. We reflect on how we can be better in the coming year. Just like you're wearing new clothes, it's also a chance to 'put on' new behaviors, like being kinder, more patient, and more helpful."

Leah and the New Clothes

Leah listened carefully, realizing that her mother was right. She loved her new dress, but she also wanted to make sure that she was a better person in the new year. As she thought about the past year, she remembered moments when she had argued with her younger brother, times when she had been impatient, and times when she hadn't listened to her parents.

"I want to be better," Leah said thoughtfully. "I want to be kinder to my brother and help out more at home."

Her mother smiled and hugged her. "That's a wonderful goal, Leah. And just like you're excited to wear your new dress, you can be excited to start fresh with your actions too."

When Rosh Hashanah arrived, Leah wore her new dress with pride. As she walked into the synagogue, she received many compliments from her friends and family. But Leah knew that the real change wasn't just in her appearance; it was in her heart.

Throughout the holiday, Leah made a special effort to be more patient and helpful. She played with her brother without complaining, helped her mother set the table, and listened carefully during the prayers. Each time she made a positive choice, she felt as proud as she did when she put on her new dress.

Leah and the New Clothes

By the end of Rosh Hashanah, Leah realized that starting fresh wasn't just about wearing new clothes—it was about making new choices and becoming a better person. She promised herself that she would continue to work on these changes throughout the year, knowing that true beauty comes from within.

Moral: A new beginning is not just about how we look, but about how we choose to act and treat others, making positive changes from the inside out.

CHAPTER SEVEN

Nathan and the Golden Coin

One sunny afternoon, Nathan was playing in the park near his home when something shiny caught his eye. He bent down and discovered a golden coin half-buried in the dirt. Excited by his discovery, Nathan carefully picked up the coin and held it up to the sunlight. It gleamed brightly, and he wondered how it had ended up there.

Nathan couldn't wait to show the coin to his parents. He ran home, his heart pounding with excitement, imagining all the things he could buy with such a treasure. When he burst through the door, his mother was in the kitchen preparing for Rosh Hashanah.

"Look what I found, Mom!" Nathan exclaimed, holding out the golden coin.

His mother turned around and gasped. "What a beautiful coin, Nathan! It must be very special," she said, admiring its shine. "But have you thought about what you might do with it?"

Nathan thought for a moment. "I was thinking I could buy something fun with it," he admitted. "Maybe a toy or some candy."

Nathan and the Golden Coin

His mother smiled and sat down beside him. "That's one idea," she said. "But with Rosh Hashanah coming up, perhaps there's something even more meaningful you could do with it. Rosh Hashanah is a time for new beginnings and for thinking about how we can be better people in the year ahead. One way to do that is by helping others."

Nathan listened carefully, intrigued by his mother's words. "What do you mean, help others?" he asked.

"Well," his mother replied, "there are many people who might not have as much as we do, especially during the holidays. You could use your coin to bring joy to someone who needs it."

Nathan considered this, realizing that his golden coin could indeed do more than just buy him something for himself. After a few moments, he made up his mind. "I want to use the coin to help someone," he decided. "But how can I do that?"

His mother suggested they visit the local store to buy food for a family in need. Together, they walked to the store and used the golden coin to purchase a variety of foods that would be perfect for a Rosh Hashanah meal. Nathan felt proud as he handed over the coin, knowing that it was going to make someone else's holiday special.

Nathan and the Golden Coin

Later that day, Nathan and his mother delivered the food to a family in their community who had recently fallen on hard times. The family was overjoyed and deeply touched by the gesture. Nathan's heart swelled with happiness as he saw the smiles on their faces.

As they walked home, Nathan realized that the golden coin had brought him more joy through giving than it ever could have through buying a toy or candy. He understood that the true value of the coin wasn't in its material worth but in the happiness it had brought to others.

Moral: Sharing our blessings with others brings true happiness and fulfillment, making the world a kinder place.

CHAPTER EIGHT

Tzipora and Baking Challah

Tzipora loved helping her mother in the kitchen, especially when it came to baking challah for Rosh Hashanah. The smell of fresh bread filled the house, creating a warm and inviting atmosphere that Tzipora cherished. Every Friday, she and her mother would bake challah, but the challah for Rosh Hashanah was extra special—it was sweet, round, and symbolic of the hope for a full and prosperous year ahead.

As the holiday approached, Tzipora was eager to help with the baking. Early one morning, she joined her mother in the kitchen, ready to start the process. The ingredients were laid out on the counter: flour, yeast, sugar, eggs, and a jar of golden honey. Tzipora watched as her mother began to mix the dough, and soon she was kneading it alongside her, feeling the sticky, smooth texture under her fingers.

"Why do we make round challah for Rosh Hashanah, Mom?" Tzipora asked as they worked.

Tzipora and Baking Challah

Her mother smiled and explained, "The round shape of the challah represents the cycle of the year—how it has no beginning and no end. It's a reminder that life is continuous and that every year we have a chance to start fresh, to improve, and to grow. The sweetness of the challah, with the added honey, symbolizes our wish for a sweet new year."

Tzipora nodded, understanding the significance behind the challah. As they shaped the dough into round loaves, she thought about the past year and what she hoped for in the year to come. She wanted to be more patient with her younger brother, to help more around the house, and to be a better friend.

As the dough rose and the loaves took shape, Tzipora's excitement grew. She carefully brushed the tops with egg wash and sprinkled sesame seeds on top, just as her mother had taught her. Together, they placed the loaves in the oven, and soon the house was filled with the rich, comforting aroma of baking bread.

When the challah was finally ready, Tzipora couldn't wait to share it with her family. She helped set the table, placing the round loaves in the center as a symbol of the new year. That evening, as the family gathered for their Rosh Hashanah meal, they said the blessings over the challah, each member taking a piece and dipping it in honey.

Tzipora and Baking Challah

As they enjoyed the sweet, soft bread, Tzipora felt a deep sense of satisfaction. The challah was more than just food; it was a symbol of the love and togetherness that filled their home. She realized that baking the challah with her mother had not only brought them closer but had also connected them to the traditions and hopes of the holiday.

For Tzipora, the round challah represented the circle of life, family, and the endless possibilities of a new year. She knew that each year, they would gather around the table, share the challah, and celebrate the bonds that made their family strong.

Moral: Cooking and preparing food together strengthens family bonds and brings warmth and meaning to the traditions we cherish.

CHAPTER NINE

Israel and the New Beginning

Israel was both excited and nervous as Rosh Hashanah approached. This year was particularly special because it marked the start of a new chapter in his life—he was about to start at a new school. Israel had always been friendly and outgoing, but the thought of meeting new people and making new friends in a different environment filled him with a mixture of excitement and anxiety.

The night before his first day at the new school, Israel could hardly sleep. He kept thinking about all the things that could go wrong. What if no one liked him? What if he couldn't find his way around? What if he didn't make any friends? These thoughts swirled around in his mind, making it hard for him to rest.

The next morning, Israel's father noticed that he seemed unusually quiet. "Are you worried about starting at the new school?" his father asked gently.

Israel nodded, his stomach fluttering with nerves. "What if I don't fit in, Dad?" he asked, voicing his fears.

Israel and the New Beginning

His father smiled reassuringly. "Starting something new can be scary, but remember that Rosh Hashanah is all about new beginnings. Just like the new year gives us a chance to start fresh, starting at a new school is an opportunity to meet new people, learn new things, and grow. Think of it as an adventure."

Israel considered his father's words. He had always loved adventures, and maybe this new school could be just that—an adventure in making new friends and discovering new possibilities. With his father's encouragement, he decided to approach the day with a positive attitude.

When Israel arrived at the school, he felt a little overwhelmed by all the new faces and the unfamiliar surroundings. But he took a deep breath and reminded himself of what his father had said. He walked up to a group of kids who were chatting near the entrance and introduced himself. "Hi, I'm Israel. I'm new here. Can I join you?"

The other kids smiled and welcomed him into their group. They introduced themselves and showed him around the school, helping him find his classroom and navigate the hallways. By the time lunch rolled around, Israel felt much more at ease. He had already made a few friends and was starting to feel like he belonged.

Israel and the New Beginning

As the school day ended, Israel walked home with a bounce in his step. He couldn't wait to tell his parents about all the new friends he had made and the things he had learned. That evening, as they gathered for the Rosh Hashanah meal, Israel shared his experiences with pride.

He realized that his father had been right—starting at a new school was a new beginning, just like the new year. It was an opportunity to embrace change, meet new people, and learn new things. Israel felt a renewed sense of confidence and excitement for the future, knowing that he could handle whatever challenges came his way.

Moral: Every new beginning is an opportunity to grow, learn, and make new friends, embracing change with courage and optimism.

CHAPTER TEN

Ruth and the Apple with Honey

Ruth loved everything about Rosh Hashanah, especially the sweet tradition of dipping apples in honey. Each year, she eagerly awaited the moment when her family would gather around the table, say the blessings, and share the delicious combination of crisp apples and golden honey. It was her favorite part of the holiday, a moment that made her feel warm and connected to her family.

This year, as Rosh Hashanah approached, Ruth found herself wondering why they dipped apples in honey. She knew it was a tradition, but she wanted to understand the deeper meaning behind it. One afternoon, she decided to ask her grandmother, who always seemed to have the answers to her questions.

Ruth's grandmother was sitting in the garden, knitting a scarf, when Ruth approached her. "Grandma," Ruth began, "why do we dip apples in honey on Rosh Hashanah? I know it's a tradition, but what does it really mean?"

Ruth and the Apple with Honey

Her grandmother smiled and put down her knitting. "That's a wonderful question, Ruth," she said, patting the seat beside her. "The apple and honey are symbols of our hopes for the new year. The apple represents good health and a fruitful life, while the honey symbolizes the sweetness we wish for in the coming year. When we dip the apple in honey, we're not just enjoying a tasty treat—we're expressing our desire for a year filled with good things."

Ruth listened carefully, absorbing her grandmother's words. "So it's like making a wish for the new year?" she asked.

"Exactly," her grandmother replied. "It's a way of bringing sweetness into our lives and the lives of those we love. But remember, Ruth, the sweetness we wish for isn't just about what we eat. It's also about how we treat others and the kindness we show. When we're kind and loving, we bring sweetness into the world."

Ruth thought about this as she picked up an apple from the basket beside her grandmother. She realized that the simple act of dipping an apple in honey held a much deeper meaning. It wasn't just about enjoying a delicious snack; it was about committing to a year of kindness, love, and sweetness in all her actions.

Ruth and the Apple with Honey

That evening, as her family gathered for the Rosh Hashanah meal, Ruth couldn't wait to share what she had learned. She carefully dipped her apple in honey and, before taking a bite, made a silent wish for the new year. She wished for good health for her family, success in school, and, most importantly, the strength to be kind and bring sweetness into the lives of others.

As she enjoyed the sweet taste of the apple and honey, Ruth felt a deep sense of peace and happiness. She knew that the true sweetness of Rosh Hashanah came not just from the honey, but from the love and kindness they shared as a family.

From that day on, Ruth made it her goal to spread sweetness wherever she went. Whether it was helping a friend, being patient with her siblings, or simply offering a smile, Ruth understood that every act of kindness made the world a little bit sweeter.

Moral: Sweetness comes not just from what we eat, but from the kindness we show to others, making the world a better place.

CHAPTER ELEVEN

Moses and the Shofar

Moses had always been fascinated by the shofar, the ram's horn that was blown during Rosh Hashanah to mark the beginning of the Jewish New Year. The powerful, haunting sound of the shofar resonated deep within him, and every year, he eagerly waited for the moment when it would be blown in the synagogue. This year, however, Moses was determined to do more than just listen—he wanted to learn how to blow the shofar himself.

Moses' grandfather, who had been the shofar blower in their synagogue for many years, agreed to teach him. One day after school, Moses visited his grandfather's house, where they sat together in the cozy living room. His grandfather gently handed him the shofar and explained the significance of its sound. "The shofar is more than just an instrument," his grandfather began. "Its sound is meant to wake us up, to remind us to reflect on the past year and to inspire us to be better in the year to come. It's a call to our hearts and souls."

Moses nodded, understanding that learning to blow the shofar was not just about making noise; it was about connecting with something much deeper. With great anticipation, he raised the shofar to his lips and blew as hard as he could. But instead of a powerful blast, all that came out was a faint, sputtering sound. Moses tried again, but the result was the same—a weak, almost inaudible noise.

Moses and the Shofar

Frustrated, Moses lowered the shofar and looked at his grandfather. "It's harder than I thought," he admitted.

His grandfather smiled kindly. "It takes practice, Moses. Blowing the shofar requires not just strength, but also control and patience. The sound will come when you're ready, and when your heart is fully in it."

Moses was determined not to give up. Every day after school, he returned to his grandfather's house to practice. At first, it was difficult. The shofar felt awkward in his hands, and no matter how hard he tried, he couldn't produce the strong, clear sound he hoped for. But Moses was persistent. He practiced over and over, listening carefully to his grandfather's advice and adjusting his technique.

As the days passed, Moses noticed a change. The sound of the shofar began to improve. It grew louder, more resonant, and more powerful. Each time he blew the shofar, he felt a connection to something greater, as if the sound was coming not just from his lips, but from his heart.

Finally, on the eve of Rosh Hashanah, Moses blew into the shofar and a clear, strong sound filled the room. His grandfather beamed with pride. "You've done it, Moses!" he exclaimed. "You're ready."

Moses and the Shofar

On Rosh Hashanah, Moses stood beside his grandfather in the synagogue, holding the shofar in his hands. When the time came, he took a deep breath, closed his eyes, and blew the shofar with all his might. The powerful, stirring sound echoed through the synagogue, filling the hearts of everyone present with a sense of awe and reflection.

As Moses lowered the shofar, he saw the looks of gratitude and inspiration on the faces of those around him. He realized that the shofar had indeed fulfilled its purpose—it had awakened their hearts and souls to the new year, reminding them to reflect, to repent, and to renew their commitment to living better lives.

Moses smiled, knowing that he had not only learned how to blow the shofar, but also how to connect with the true spirit of Rosh Hashanah.

Moral: Persistence, patience, and a heartfelt connection to our actions can help us achieve our goals and make a meaningful impact.

CHAPTER TWELVE

Gila and the Golden Leaves

As the days grew cooler and the leaves began to change color, Gila knew that Rosh Hashanah was just around the corner. It was her favorite time of year, not just because of the holiday celebrations, but because of the beauty that autumn brought to the world. The trees in her village were dressed in vibrant shades of red, orange, and gold, and Gila loved to collect the fallen leaves to decorate her home.

One crisp afternoon, Gila decided to take a walk through the nearby forest to gather leaves for Rosh Hashanah. As she wandered through the trees, she marveled at the colors around her. The forest floor was covered in a blanket of leaves, each one more beautiful than the last. Gila carefully selected the most perfect leaves she could find—bright red maples, golden oaks, and fiery orange birches—and placed them in her basket.

As she collected the leaves, Gila began to think about the meaning of Rosh Hashanah. She remembered how her parents had explained that it was a time for new beginnings, a chance to reflect on the past year and to set intentions for the year to come. The idea of starting fresh resonated with her, especially as she looked at the golden leaves that symbolized the changing of the seasons.

Gila and the Golden Leaves

When Gila returned home, she spread the leaves out on the kitchen table and began to arrange them into a beautiful centerpiece for the holiday table. As she worked, her mother came into the room and admired her creation. "These leaves are so beautiful, Gila," her mother said. "They remind me of the cycle of life and the changes that come with each new year."

Gila looked up at her mother, intrigued. "What do you mean, the cycle of life?" she asked.

Her mother sat down beside her and picked up a golden leaf. "Just like the leaves change color and fall from the trees, we also go through changes in our lives. Rosh Hashanah is a time to think about those changes and to decide how we want to grow in the coming year. The golden leaves symbolize the beauty of those changes and the opportunities they bring."

Gila thought about her mother's words as she finished arranging the leaves. She realized that just as the leaves changed with the seasons, she too had the ability to change and grow. She could choose to be more patient with her younger sister, more helpful around the house, and more kind to her friends.

Gila and the Golden Leaves

As Rosh Hashanah arrived, Gila felt a deep sense of connection to the holiday. During the family meal, she proudly showed off her leaf centerpiece and shared what she had learned with her family. Together, they reflected on the changes they had experienced over the past year and the goals they wanted to set for the year ahead.

Gila knew that the golden leaves were more than just decorations—they were a reminder that change was a natural and beautiful part of life. And just like the leaves, she was ready to embrace the new year with a sense of hope and determination.

Moral: Change is a natural and beautiful part of life, bringing new opportunities for growth and improvement, just like the changing seasons.

CHAPTER THIRTEEN

Isaac and Tashlich with Friends

Isaac always looked forward to Rosh Hashanah, not just for the delicious meals and festive gatherings, but for the special tradition of Tashlich. Each year, on the afternoon of Rosh Hashanah, Isaac and his family would walk to the nearby river to perform the Tashlich ceremony. It was a time to reflect on the past year, to cast away their mistakes, and to make a fresh start.

This year, Isaac was especially excited because he had invited his friends to join him for Tashlich. They had never participated in the ceremony before, and Isaac was eager to share the experience with them. On the afternoon of Rosh Hashanah, Isaac and his friends gathered at his house, each carrying a small bag of breadcrumbs.

As they walked to the river, Isaac explained the meaning of Tashlich to his friends. "Tashlich is a tradition where we throw breadcrumbs into the water," he said. "The breadcrumbs represent our mistakes and the things we want to leave behind in the past year. By throwing them into the river, we're letting go of those mistakes and making a promise to do better in the new year."

Isaac and Tashlich with Friends

His friends listened intently, intrigued by the idea. When they arrived at the river, they found a quiet spot by the water's edge. Isaac's parents stood nearby, giving the children space to reflect on their own.

Isaac took out his bag of breadcrumbs and held it in his hand. As he looked at the river, he thought about the times he had been impatient, the arguments he had with his sister, and the moments when he had been less than kind to his friends. He knew that these were the things he wanted to let go of.

One by one, Isaac began to throw the breadcrumbs into the river. As they floated away, he felt a sense of relief, as if a weight was being lifted from his shoulders. He knew that the mistakes of the past year were now behind him, carried away by the flowing water.

Isaac's friends followed his lead, each of them tossing their breadcrumbs into the river with thoughtful expressions. After they had finished, they all stood quietly by the water, watching the river carry their mistakes away.

Isaac and Tashlich with Friends

When the ceremony was over, Isaac felt a renewed sense of hope and determination. He knew that the new year was a chance to start fresh, to be a better friend, a better brother, and a better person. As they walked back to the village, Isaac and his friends talked about their hopes and goals for the coming year, sharing their thoughts and encouraging each other to do their best.

That evening, as Isaac's family gathered for the Rosh Hashanah meal, he felt grateful for the support and friendship that surrounded him. He knew that with the help of his friends and family, he could achieve his goals and make the new year a time of growth and positive change.

Moral: Friendship and support help us let go of the past and face the future with confidence, making new beginnings even more meaningful.

CHAPTER FOURTEEN

Noa and the Little Apology

Noa was a bright and cheerful girl who loved spending time with her friends. But as Rosh Hashanah approached, something was weighing on her mind. A few weeks earlier, she had accidentally broken her best friend's favorite toy during a playdate. At the time, she hadn't told her friend what had happened, hoping that no one would notice. But now, the guilt was becoming too much to bear.

Noa knew that Rosh Hashanah was a time for reflection and making amends, and she couldn't stop thinking about the broken toy. She knew she needed to apologize, but the thought of admitting her mistake made her stomach twist with anxiety. What if her friend was angry? What if she didn't forgive her?

One evening, Noa's mother noticed that she seemed unusually quiet. "Is something bothering you, Noa?" her mother asked gently.

Noa hesitated, then nodded. "I did something wrong, and I'm afraid to tell my friend," she admitted. She explained what had happened with the toy and how she had kept it a secret.

Noa and the Little Apology

Her mother listened carefully and then hugged her. "It's never easy to admit when we've made a mistake," she said. "But Rosh Hashanah is the perfect time to apologize and make things right. It's a chance to start the new year with a clean slate. I'm sure your friend will appreciate your honesty."

Noa knew her mother was right. She took a deep breath and decided that the next day, she would visit her friend and apologize. Even though she was nervous, she knew it was the right thing to do.

The next afternoon, Noa walked to her friend's house, her heart pounding in her chest. When her friend opened the door, Noa's hands trembled, but she gathered her courage. "I need to tell you something," she began. "A few weeks ago, I accidentally broke your toy. I'm really sorry, and I should have told you right away."

Her friend looked surprised but then smiled softly. "It's okay, Noa. I was sad about the toy, but I'm glad you told me the truth. We can always fix the toy or find a new one. Our friendship is more important."

Noa and the Little Apology

Relief washed over Noa as she realized that her friend had forgiven her. They hugged, and Noa felt a weight lift off her shoulders. She knew that the honesty and apology had made their friendship even stronger.

That evening, as Noa's family celebrated Rosh Hashanah, she felt a deep sense of peace. She had faced her mistake, apologized, and made things right. Noa knew that the new year was a chance to be a better friend and to always choose honesty, even when it was difficult.

Moral: Apologizing for our mistakes helps heal relationships and brings peace, making the new year a time for fresh starts and stronger connections.

CHAPTER FIFTEEN

Aviva and the Sweet Honey

Aviva loved the taste of honey, especially during Rosh Hashanah. The tradition of dipping apples in honey was her favorite part of the holiday, and she always looked forward to the sweet treat. But this year, as the holiday approached, Aviva found herself wondering about the meaning behind the tradition. She wanted to understand why honey was so important during Rosh Hashanah.

One day, Aviva asked her grandfather, who had always been the storyteller in the family, to explain the significance of honey during the holiday. They sat together on the porch, enjoying the late afternoon sun, as her grandfather began to speak.

"Honey is special, Aviva, because it represents the sweetness we hope for in the new year," her grandfather explained. "When we dip the apple in honey, we're expressing our wish for a year filled with joy, health, and good fortune. But the honey also reminds us that life isn't always easy. Just as bees work hard to make honey, we must also work hard to bring sweetness into our lives and the lives of others."

Aviva and the Sweet Honey

Aviva listened carefully, realizing that the honey was more than just a delicious treat. It was a symbol of hope and positivity, a reminder to focus on the good things in life and to spread that goodness to others.

Her grandfather continued, "Rosh Hashanah is a time for reflection and renewal. It's a time to think about how we can be better in the coming year, how we can be kinder, more patient, and more loving. The honey encourages us to look for the sweetness in every situation, even when things are difficult."

Aviva thought about her grandfather's words as she dipped an apple slice into the honey. She realized that the tradition was not just about enjoying the taste but about setting an intention for the new year. She wanted to be like the bees, working hard to bring sweetness and positivity into her life and the lives of those around her.

That evening, as her family gathered for the Rosh Hashanah meal, Aviva felt a new sense of purpose. She made a silent promise to herself to focus on the positive and to spread kindness wherever she could. She decided to share the honey with her friends and neighbors, baking honey cakes to give as gifts and spreading the message of sweetness and hope.

Aviva and the Sweet Honey

As Aviva delivered the honey cakes to her neighbors, she felt a deep sense of joy. The smiles on their faces were even sweeter than the honey itself. She knew that by sharing the honey and the message it carried, she was making a difference in their lives.

When the holiday was over, Aviva continued to carry the lesson of the honey with her throughout the year. She looked for the sweetness in every situation, even when things were tough, and she made a conscious effort to spread kindness and positivity to everyone she met.

Moral: Sweetness comes from having a positive attitude and finding the good in every situation, just like honey brings sweetness to our lives.

CHAPTER SIXTEEN

Samuel and the Big Dinner

Samuel was eagerly helping his family prepare for the big Rosh Hashanah dinner. The kitchen was a hive of activity, with pots bubbling on the stove, fresh challah cooling on the counter, and the sweet smell of honey and spices filling the air. Samuel loved this time of year, not just because of the delicious food, but because of the sense of togetherness that the holiday brought to his family.

As the youngest in the family, Samuel was often given small tasks to help with the preparations. This year, however, he wanted to do something special to contribute to the meal. He asked his mother if there was anything extra he could do, and she smiled warmly at his enthusiasm.

"Why don't you help set the table, Samuel?" she suggested. "You can choose the decorations and make it look beautiful for our guests."

Samuel was thrilled. He carefully selected the best dishes, polished the silverware, and placed candles in the center of the table. He then went outside to pick fresh flowers from the garden, arranging them in a vase as the finishing touch. The table looked elegant and welcoming, and Samuel felt a surge of pride knowing that he had played a part in making the dinner special.

Samuel and the Big Dinner

As the sun began to set, family and friends started to arrive, filling the house with laughter and conversation. Samuel's father welcomed everyone, and they gathered around the beautifully set table. Before they began the meal, Samuel's father raised his glass and said, "Rosh Hashanah is a time to celebrate new beginnings and to reflect on the blessings we've received. It's also a time to be thankful for the love and support of our family and friends. This dinner is a reminder of the importance of coming together, sharing our joys, and looking forward to the year ahead."

Samuel listened intently, feeling a warm sense of connection to everyone in the room. He realized that the dinner was about more than just the food—it was about the love and togetherness that came from sharing a meal with the people who mattered most. The effort he had put into setting the table was a way of showing his appreciation for his family and guests, and it made the meal even more meaningful.

As the evening continued, Samuel noticed how everyone lingered at the table, enjoying the food and each other's company. The stories shared, the laughter, and the blessings made the evening feel magical. Samuel felt proud to be part of something so special, knowing that his contributions had helped create a warm and welcoming atmosphere.

Samuel and the Big Dinner

When the meal finally came to an end, Samuel's mother pulled him aside and gave him a big hug. "You did a wonderful job tonight, Samuel," she said. "The table looked beautiful, and your efforts made everyone feel welcome and loved."

Samuel beamed with pride, knowing that he had helped make the Rosh Hashanah dinner a night to remember. As he went to bed that night, he thought about the true meaning of the holiday. It wasn't just about the food; it was about the love and connection that came from gathering together and sharing in the joy of the new year.

Moral: Celebrating together with loved ones strengthens family bonds and brings joy to the holiday, making every effort meaningful.

CHAPTER SEVENTEEN

Hannah and the Lost Apple

Hannah was excited as she joined her family in the orchard to pick apples for Rosh Hashanah. The orchard was filled with trees heavy with fruit, their branches bending under the weight of the bright red apples. Hannah loved this annual tradition, knowing that the apples they picked would soon be dipped in honey, a sweet symbol of the new year.

As she wandered through the rows of trees, Hannah searched for the perfect apple. She wanted one that was shiny, red, and just the right size. Finally, after carefully inspecting several trees, she found it—a beautiful apple hanging high on a branch. She reached up on her tiptoes, stretching as far as she could, and just as her fingers brushed the apple, it slipped from the branch and fell into the bushes below.

Hannah's heart sank as she watched the apple disappear into the thick foliage. She crouched down and began searching through the bushes, pushing aside leaves and twigs in an attempt to find the apple. But no matter how hard she looked, it seemed to have vanished.

Hannah and the Lost Apple

Frustrated and on the verge of tears, Hannah sat back on her heels. She had been so excited to find the perfect apple, and now it was gone. But then she remembered something her father had told her earlier that day: "Sometimes the best things take time to find, Hannah. You just have to be patient and keep looking."

Taking a deep breath, Hannah decided not to give up. She stood up and carefully began searching again, this time moving slowly and methodically. She pushed aside each branch, checking every nook and cranny. Finally, after what felt like an eternity, she spotted a glimmer of red through the leaves. With a burst of excitement, Hannah reached into the bushes and pulled out the apple. It was even more beautiful than she had remembered, shining in the sunlight as if it had been waiting just for her.

Hannah felt a surge of pride as she held the apple in her hands. Her patience and determination had paid off. She ran back to her family, eager to show them her prize. "I found it!" she exclaimed, her face glowing with happiness.

Hannah and the Lost Apple

That evening, as the family gathered for the Rosh Hashanah meal, Hannah proudly placed her apple on the table. They dipped it in honey, savoring the sweet taste and the meaning behind the tradition. As Hannah took her first bite, she realized that the apple tasted even better because of the effort she had put into finding it.

The experience taught Hannah an important lesson: sometimes, the things that are most valuable require patience and perseverance. She knew that this lesson would stay with her throughout the new year, reminding her that good things come to those who don't give up.

Moral: Patience and determination help us achieve our goals, making the reward even sweeter when we finally succeed.

CHAPTER EIGHTEEN

Jonah and the Night Lights

Jonah loved the nights of Rosh Hashanah when his family would gather to light candles and welcome the new year. There was something magical about the way the soft, flickering light filled their home, casting a warm glow over everything. The candles seemed to hold a special kind of energy, one that made Jonah feel calm and hopeful for the year ahead.

One evening, as they were preparing to light the candles, Jonah asked his mother about the tradition. "Why do we light candles on Rosh Hashanah?" he asked, curious to understand the meaning behind the ritual.

His mother smiled and sat down beside him. "The candles represent the light that we bring into the world," she explained. "Each flame is a symbol of hope, renewal, and the possibility of a better future. When we light the candles, we're not just illuminating our home — we're also bringing light into our lives and the lives of others."

Jonah and the Night Lights

Jonah listened intently, thinking about the significance of the candles. He had always loved the way they looked, but now he realized they held a deeper meaning. The light of the candles was a reminder to be kind, to help others, and to bring positivity into the world.

As they lit the candles that night, Jonah felt a sense of responsibility. He wanted to be a source of light for others, just like the candles were for his family. He made a silent promise to himself to spread kindness and to be a positive influence in the lives of those around him.

After the candles were lit, the family gathered around the table to share their hopes and dreams for the new year. Jonah's father spoke about the importance of community and the role each person played in making the world a better place. "Just as these candles light up our home," he said, "we can all bring light into the world through our actions. It's up to each of us to make the new year brighter for everyone."

Jonah took his father's words to heart. Over the next few days, he looked for opportunities to be helpful and kind. He helped his younger sister with her homework, offered to do extra chores around the house, and made an effort to be patient and understanding with his friends.

Jonah and the Night Lights

Each time he did something kind, Jonah thought about the candles and the light they represented. He realized that being a source of light didn't always mean doing something big—sometimes, it was the small acts of kindness that made the biggest difference.

As the new year began, Jonah continued to focus on bringing light into the world. He knew that by being kind, helpful, and positive, he could make a difference in the lives of those around him, just like the candles lit up their home on Rosh Hashanah.

Moral: We can bring light and hope into the world through our kindness and actions, making every day a little brighter for those around us.

CHAPTER NINETEEN

Ziva and the Festival of Lights

Ziva loved Rosh Hashanah for many reasons—the delicious food, the time spent with family, and the excitement of the new year. But her favorite part of the holiday was the lighting of the candles. There was something magical about the way the candles transformed their home, filling it with warmth and light, and creating a sense of peace and hope for the year ahead.

On the first night of Rosh Hashanah, Ziva helped her mother prepare the candles. She carefully placed them in the candleholders, making sure each one was straight and secure. As she did, she thought about the significance of the candles and what they meant for the holiday.

"Why do we light candles on Rosh Hashanah, Mom?" Ziva asked, her curiosity getting the better of her.

Her mother paused and smiled. "The candles are a symbol of the light we bring into the world," she explained. "Rosh Hashanah is a time for new beginnings, and the candles represent our hopes for a bright and positive future. Each flame is a reminder that even in the darkest times, there is always light and hope."

Ziva and the Festival of Lights

Ziva listened carefully, realizing that the candles were more than just a decoration. They were a powerful symbol of the hope and positivity that Rosh Hashanah brought to her family and to the world. She wanted to make sure that the light of the candles would shine brightly, not just in their home, but in her actions throughout the year.

As they lit the candles that night, Ziva felt a deep sense of connection to the tradition. She watched the flames flicker and dance, casting a warm glow over the room. It was a moment of quiet reflection, a time to think about the year that had passed and to set intentions for the year ahead.

Ziva's father spoke about the importance of bringing light into the world, not just during Rosh Hashanah, but every day. "The light of these candles is a reminder that we all have the power to make the world a better place," he said. "By being kind, compassionate, and positive, we can spread light and hope to those around us."

Ziva took her father's words to heart. She decided that in the coming year, she would focus on being a source of light for others. Whether it was through small acts of kindness, helping a friend in need, or simply offering a smile, Ziva knew that every positive action could make a difference.

Ziva and the Festival of Lights

Throughout the holiday, Ziva made a conscious effort to be kind and helpful. She helped her mother in the kitchen, played with her younger brother, and even reached out to a classmate who seemed lonely. Each time she did something kind, she thought about the candles and the light they represented.

As the new year began, Ziva continued to focus on bringing light into the world. She knew that by being a positive influence, she could make the world a better place, just like the candles had filled her home with warmth and hope on Rosh Hashanah.

Moral: Bringing light and positivity into the world makes it a better place for everyone, and each of us has the power to spread that light through our actions.

CHAPTER TWENTY

Rafi and the Honey Bees

Rafi had always been fascinated by the bees that buzzed around his family's garden, especially during the summer months. He loved watching them as they flitted from flower to flower, collecting nectar to make honey. But it wasn't until Rosh Hashanah approached that Rafi began to truly appreciate the hard work of the bees and the significance of the honey they produced.

One day, as the holiday neared, Rafi's father suggested they visit a local beekeeper to learn more about how honey was made. Rafi was excited about the idea and eagerly agreed. They drove to a nearby farm where the beekeeper, Mr. Goldstein, welcomed them warmly and invited them to see the beehives.

As they approached the hives, Rafi could hear the low hum of the bees at work. Mr. Goldstein explained how the bees collected nectar from the flowers and brought it back to the hive, where they turned it into honey. "Bees are small, but they work together to create something sweet and valuable," Mr. Goldstein said. "Each drop of honey represents the hard work and cooperation of many bees."

Rafi and the Honey Bees

Rafi listened with fascination, realizing just how much effort went into making the honey that his family enjoyed every year during Rosh Hashanah. The beekeeper continued, "Honey is a symbol of the sweetness we hope for in the new year. It reminds us that while life may have its challenges, we can still find joy and sweetness if we work hard and support each other."

As they walked around the farm, Mr. Goldstein showed Rafi the honeycombs inside the hives, explaining how the bees stored the honey and protected it. Rafi was amazed by the intricate work of the bees and how each one played a crucial role in the hive. He realized that, just like the bees, people could achieve great things when they worked together and supported one another.

When they returned home, Rafi couldn't stop thinking about the bees and the honey they produced. He understood now why honey was such an important part of Rosh Hashanah—it wasn't just about the sweet taste, but about the hard work, cooperation, and perseverance that it represented.

Rafi and the Honey Bees

That evening, as Rafi's family gathered to celebrate Rosh Hashanah, they dipped apples in honey and shared the traditional blessings. Rafi felt a deeper connection to the ritual this year, knowing the story behind the honey. He made a promise to himself to work hard in the coming year, to be a good friend, and to help others whenever he could.

Throughout the holiday, Rafi thought about the bees and how their teamwork created something so sweet and valuable. He knew that by working together and supporting each other, he and his family could make the new year a time of joy and success.

As the year progressed, Rafi carried the lesson of the honey bees with him. He worked hard in school, helped his parents around the house, and always looked for ways to support his friends. He knew that just like the bees, he could make a difference in the world by contributing his best efforts and by being there for others.

Moral: Hard work and teamwork create sweet and valuable results, just like the bees and their honey, reminding us of the importance of cooperation and perseverance.

CHAPTER TWENTY-ONE

Esther and the Return Home

Esther had been away at school for what felt like forever, and as Rosh Hashanah approached, she couldn't wait to return home to her family. The thought of being surrounded by her loved ones, sharing in the holiday traditions, and enjoying the comfort of her childhood home filled her with excitement. There was something special about Rosh Hashanah that made Esther feel connected to her roots, and this year, she felt the pull of home even more strongly.

The day finally arrived when Esther boarded the train that would take her back to her village. As the landscape whizzed by, her heart swelled with anticipation. She thought about the warm embrace of her parents, the laughter of her younger siblings, and the smell of her mother's cooking filling the house. There was nothing like the feeling of coming home.

When Esther arrived at the station, she spotted her family waiting for her on the platform. Her mother's face lit up with joy, and her father's eyes twinkled with pride. Esther's younger siblings rushed to greet her, their voices bubbling with excitement as they hugged her tightly.

Esther and the Return Home

"Welcome home, Esther!" her mother said, tears of happiness in her eyes.

"It's so good to have you back," her father added, pulling her into a warm embrace.

Esther felt a wave of emotion wash over her. Being home for Rosh Hashanah was exactly what she needed. The worries and stresses of school seemed to melt away in the presence of her family, and she knew that this was where she truly belonged.

As they walked home together, Esther noticed how the village had changed since she had been away. The trees were beginning to change color, signaling the arrival of autumn, and there was a crispness in the air that she associated with the holiday season. It was as if the whole world was preparing for a fresh start, just like she was.

That evening, as they gathered around the table for the Rosh Hashanah meal, Esther's father spoke about the importance of family and the joy of being together for the holiday. "Rosh Hashanah is a time for new beginnings, but it's also a time to reconnect with the people who matter most," he said. "No matter where we go or what we do, our family is our foundation. It's the place where we find love, support, and belonging."

Esther and the Return Home

Esther looked around the table at the faces of her loved ones and felt a deep sense of gratitude. She knew that her family was her anchor, the source of her strength and happiness. The past year had been challenging, with the demands of school and the distance from home, but being back with her family reminded her of what truly mattered.

As they dipped apples in honey and shared the blessings for the new year, Esther made a silent promise to herself. She vowed to cherish her family, to stay connected no matter where life took her, and to always return home for Rosh Hashanah. The holiday was a reminder that no matter how far she traveled, her family would always be her home, the place where she was loved and accepted unconditionally.

The warmth and love that filled the room that evening stayed with Esther long after the holiday ended. She carried it with her as she returned to school, knowing that no matter how far she went, her family would always be there for her, waiting to welcome her back home.

Moral: Family is a source of love and support, and no matter where life takes us, returning home reminds us of what truly matters.

CHAPTER TWENTY-TWO

Yael and the New Year's Wishes

As Rosh Hashanah approached, Yael was excited about all the holiday traditions, but there was one she looked forward to the most—writing New Year's wishes for her family. Every year, Yael's family had a special tradition where they would write down their hopes and dreams for the coming year on small pieces of paper and place them in a special box. Then, on the first night of Rosh Hashanah, they would read them aloud and share their wishes with each other.

This year, Yael was determined to write the perfect wishes for her family. She wanted each one to be thoughtful and meaningful, something that would inspire and uplift her loved ones as they entered the new year. She spent hours sitting at her desk, thinking carefully about what to write.

For her father, who had been working hard at his job, she wished for success and recognition. "I wish for you to be rewarded for all your hard work, and for your efforts to be appreciated by everyone around you," she wrote.

For her mother, who always took care of everyone, she wished for peace and relaxation. "I wish for you to find time to rest and take care of yourself, just as you take care of all of us," she wrote.

Yael and the New Year's Wishes

Her younger brother, who was just starting school, she wished for confidence and happiness. "I wish for you to make new friends and enjoy every moment of learning and playing," she wrote.

And for herself, Yael wished for courage and growth. "I wish to be brave in facing new challenges, to learn from my experiences, and to become the best version of myself," she wrote.

When she had finished writing all her wishes, Yael carefully folded each piece of paper and placed them in the special box. She felt a sense of pride and anticipation, knowing that these wishes carried her hopes and dreams for the people she loved most.

On the first night of Rosh Hashanah, Yael's family gathered around the dinner table. After the meal, it was time to share their New Year's wishes. Each family member took turns reading their wishes aloud, and as they did, the room filled with love and positivity.

When it was Yael's turn, she opened the box and read her wishes one by one. Her family listened intently, their faces lighting up with smiles and tears as they heard the thoughtful words Yael had written. Each wish was a reflection of the love and care Yael had for them, and it made the moment even more special.

Yael and the New Year's Wishes

Yael's father hugged her tightly after she finished reading. "These are beautiful wishes, Yael," he said. "You've captured exactly what we all need in the coming year."

Her mother nodded in agreement. "Thank you, Yael, for putting so much thought and love into these wishes. They mean the world to us."

As the family sat together, reflecting on the wishes they had shared, Yael felt a deep sense of connection to her loved ones. She realized that the act of writing the wishes had not only brought them closer but had also set a positive tone for the new year. It was a reminder that Rosh Hashanah was a time to think about the future, to set intentions, and to support each other in achieving their dreams.

Yael knew that these wishes would guide her throughout the year, reminding her of the love and hope that surrounded her. And as she drifted off to sleep that night, she felt grateful for the opportunity to start the new year with such a strong sense of purpose and connection.

Moral: Setting intentions and expressing our hopes for the future can bring us closer to our loved ones and guide us in making the new year meaningful and fulfilling.

CHAPTER TWENTY-THREE

Uri and the Secret Tree

Uri was always up for an adventure, and there was no better place for one than the forest near his home. As Rosh Hashanah approached, Uri's parents told him that they would be spending the holiday at his grandparents' house, which was surrounded by a vast and mysterious forest. Uri couldn't wait to explore it and see what secrets it held.

On the first morning of Rosh Hashanah, Uri set out early to explore the forest. The air was crisp, and the leaves on the trees were beginning to turn shades of red, orange, and gold. Uri wandered deeper into the woods, enjoying the peaceful sounds of nature—the rustling of leaves, the chirping of birds, and the gentle breeze that whispered through the trees.

As he walked, Uri noticed something unusual in the distance. It was a tall tree, standing alone in a small clearing, its branches heavy with ripe, golden apples. The tree looked different from the others around it, almost as if it was glowing in the morning light. Curious, Uri approached the tree, feeling a sense of excitement.

Uri and the Secret Tree

When he reached the tree, Uri realized that the apples were unlike any he had ever seen before. They were perfectly round, with a deep golden color that shimmered in the sunlight. Uri reached up and picked one of the apples, marveling at its beauty. He took a bite and was surprised by the sweetness of the fruit—it was the most delicious apple he had ever tasted.

As he enjoyed the apple, Uri looked around and realized that the tree was special, almost magical. He decided that he would share these incredible apples with his family, especially since Rosh Hashanah was a time for new beginnings and blessings. Uri carefully picked several more apples and placed them in his basket.

When Uri returned to his grandparents' house, he found his family gathered in the kitchen, preparing for the holiday meal. "Look what I found!" Uri exclaimed, holding up the golden apples.

His family gathered around, admiring the apples and asking where he had found them. Uri told them about the secret tree in the forest, and they all agreed that the apples were a special gift, perfect for celebrating Rosh Hashanah.

Uri and the Secret Tree

That evening, as the family gathered for the Rosh Hashanah meal, Uri's grandmother placed the golden apples in the center of the table. They dipped the apples in honey, as was the tradition, and shared the blessings for a sweet new year. As they ate the apples, they marveled at their unique flavor and the sense of wonder that Uri's discovery had brought to the holiday.

Uri felt a deep sense of satisfaction, knowing that he had contributed something special to the celebration. The golden apples were more than just a delicious treat—they were a symbol of the magic and blessings that Rosh Hashanah brought to their lives.

As the holiday came to an end, Uri's family thanked him for finding the secret tree and bringing such joy to their Rosh Hashanah. Uri smiled, feeling proud of his adventure and the special gift he had shared with his loved ones.

From that day on, the golden apples became a cherished part of their Rosh Hashanah tradition, reminding them of the sweetness and magic that the new year could bring.

Moral: Discovering and sharing the blessings of life can bring joy and wonder to those we love, making the new year even more special.

CHAPTER TWENTY-FOUR

Rivka and the Colorful Apples

Rivka loved spending time in her family's orchard, especially as Rosh Hashanah approached. The trees were laden with ripe, juicy apples, ready to be picked and enjoyed. But this year, something unusual caught Rivka's eye. Among the familiar red and green apples, she noticed a tree with apples of many different colors—yellow, pink, even purple! Rivka had never seen such a variety of apples before, and she was eager to learn more about them.

One afternoon, Rivka's father joined her in the orchard, and she excitedly pointed out the colorful apples. "Look, Papa! Have you ever seen apples like these before?" she asked, her eyes wide with wonder.

Her father smiled and nodded. "Yes, Rivka, these are special apples. They remind me of the diversity and beauty of life. Just like these apples come in different colors, shapes, and sizes, people are also different in many ways. But it's our differences that make the world so beautiful and interesting."

Rivka listened carefully, intrigued by her father's words. She had always known that people were different, but she had never thought about how those differences could be something to celebrate.

Rivka and the Colorful Apples

"Rosh Hashanah is a time to reflect on the year that has passed and to look forward to the year ahead," her father continued. "It's also a time to appreciate the diversity around us. Just as each apple has its own unique color and flavor, each person has their own unique qualities that make them special."

Rivka thought about the people in her life—her family, her friends, and her neighbors. Each of them was different in their own way, but together, they made her life rich and full. She realized that just like the apples in the orchard, the variety of people in her life added color and flavor to her world.

As they continued to walk through the orchard, Rivka's father suggested they pick some of the colorful apples to share with the family during the Rosh Hashanah meal. "These apples will remind us of the beauty of diversity," he said. "And they'll be a symbol of our hope for a sweet and colorful new year."

Rivka eagerly agreed, and they carefully selected a variety of apples—yellow, pink, purple, and of course, the classic red and green. As they filled their basket, Rivka felt a deep sense of appreciation for the diversity around her.

Rivka and the Colorful Apples

That evening, as the family gathered for the Rosh Hashanah meal, Rivka proudly placed the colorful apples on the table. They dipped the apples in honey, savoring the sweetness and reflecting on the year that had passed. Rivka's father shared the story of the colorful apples with the family, reminding everyone of the importance of appreciating and celebrating the differences that made their lives so rich and vibrant.

As they enjoyed the meal, Rivka felt a sense of pride in her heritage and a deep appreciation for the diversity around her. She knew that the colorful apples were more than just a tasty treat—they were a symbol of the beauty and richness that diversity brought to her life.

Rivka decided that in the coming year, she would make an effort to appreciate the unique qualities of the people around her. She would celebrate their differences and recognize the beauty in diversity, just as she had with the colorful apples in the orchard.

Moral: Diversity adds color and richness to our lives, and by appreciating and celebrating our differences, we can create a more beautiful and harmonious world.

CHAPTER TWENTY-FOUR

Naomi and the New Friend

Naomi was excited about Rosh Hashanah, but she was also a little nervous. Her family had just moved to a new neighborhood, and everything felt different. She missed her old friends and the familiar streets of her previous home. The thought of celebrating Rosh Hashanah in a new place, without the friends she had grown up with, made her feel a bit lonely.

A few days before the holiday, Naomi's mother suggested that they visit the local synagogue to meet some of their new neighbors. "It's a great way to get to know people before Rosh Hashanah," her mother said. "You might even make some new friends."

Naomi wasn't sure how she felt about the idea, but she agreed to go. She knew that Rosh Hashanah was a time for new beginnings, and maybe this was an opportunity to start fresh in their new home.

When they arrived at the synagogue, Naomi was greeted by a group of children who were busy preparing for the holiday. They were decorating the sanctuary with flowers and setting up tables for the Rosh Hashanah meal. Naomi's mother introduced her to the other kids, and soon Naomi found herself helping to hang garlands of flowers.

Naomi and the New Friend

As they worked together, one of the girls, Leah, struck up a conversation with Naomi. "I'm so glad you're here!" Leah said with a smile. "I was hoping to meet someone new. Rosh Hashanah is always more fun when you have friends to celebrate with."

Naomi felt a surge of relief. Leah was friendly and welcoming, and soon they were chatting like old friends. They talked about their favorite Rosh Hashanah traditions, the foods they loved, and the new dresses they would wear for the holiday.

By the time they had finished decorating, Naomi felt much more at ease. She realized that Leah was right—Rosh Hashanah was indeed more fun when you had friends to share it with. And even though she missed her old friends, Naomi was excited about the possibility of making new ones in her new neighborhood.

On the first night of Rosh Hashanah, Naomi's family attended the holiday service at the synagogue. After the service, they joined the community for a festive meal. Naomi was thrilled when Leah invited her to sit with her family. As they dipped apples in honey and shared the blessings for the new year, Naomi felt a deep sense of belonging. She knew that this new neighborhood could become her home, and that Leah could become a close friend.

Naomi and the New Friend

As the holiday continued, Naomi and Leah spent more time together. They played games, helped their parents prepare meals, and talked about their hopes and dreams for the new year. Naomi realized that moving to a new place didn't have to be scary—it could be an opportunity to meet new people and create new memories.

By the end of Rosh Hashanah, Naomi felt more connected to her new community. She knew that she had made a friend in Leah, and that this friendship was just the beginning of her new life in the neighborhood. Naomi was grateful for the fresh start that Rosh Hashanah had given her, and she looked forward to the adventures and friendships that the new year would bring.

Moral: New beginnings can lead to new friendships and opportunities, and by being open and welcoming, we can make any place feel like home.

Dear Readers,

Our team would like to thank you sincerely for purchasing our book. Your support and interest in our work are extremely important and inspiring to us.

Your feedback is valuable to us, so We would like to ask you to share your thoughts about the book on the Amazon platform. Your honest reviews will help us better understand what your opinion is about our book and what elements can be improved or changed in the future.

We greatly appreciate every comment, whether it is positive or negative. Your feedback will help other readers make an informed choice when purchasing a book.

Best regards,
Team Judah Joy Press

Don't forget to check out other books by Judah Joy Press

Made in the USA
Las Vegas, NV
20 September 2024

95492327R10046